Human Resources

Human Resources

poems

Erin Murphy

GRAYSON BOOKS
West Hartford, Connecticut
graysonbooks.com

Contents

III

I

Imperial Valley

Large-scale production would be impossible without Mexican field labor ... costs would increase by fifty percent.

—agriculture company executive, 1927

They import gringa packers
by the cartload from Fresno,

but most of us come from
over the border, whole families

sleeping in ditch bank shacks
on tenant farms. Our niños

work the fields, too. By evening
they're sunburned and spent, dead

weight in their mothers' arms.
Early spring when the ground

is greedy with heat, we plant
cotton. Too soon and the stalks

are stunted like grown boys
who never got enough to eat.

Most farmers like fuzzy seed,
half a bushel an acre. We plant

down deep since rain comes
rarely to these parts, use our feet

to measure between each hole.
No cotton, no money, says

the boss. I translate for my wife:
Sin algodón, no dinero.

Then we turn to grapefruit—
"forbidden fruit," fruto prohibido—

keeping an eye out for pale skin
with smudges of pinkish blush.

"Kissed by the sun," they say,
besado por el sol. The heavier

the fruit, the more juice it holds,
like my wife's breasts

when they swell with milk.
Between seasons we dig silt

by hand from irrigation trenches.
In May, cantaloupe pickers

trickle down from Turlock.
By summer, we harvest blood

red tomatoes and alfalfa—
in fall, cotton and milo maize.

Come the new year, we slice heads
of lettuce straight off the stem,

one worker to a row, runners
in an all-day race against the sun.

If we fall behind, the boss man
knows—he pays gang pushers

a quarter extra per day to track
our pace. Más rápido, más rápido!

they demand, treating us more
like mulas than men. Pick, pick,

pick, pick, pick till it's time
to bury the seeds again.

Rana Plaza

Savar, Bangladesh

My father was in hospital
that day, his pulse as low as

the Bangshi during dry season.
I wanted to stay with him,

but we were warned *No time off*
for illness, not even your own.

Had he died—which, *Alhamdulillah*,
he did not—the bosses would

have said, *Nothing to be done.*
If he's dead, he's dead.

And so I left my father's side.
It was 8:10 a.m. when I arrived.

Workers gathered by the gate,
afraid. Reshma squeezed

my arm. In my mind there is
a photograph of her wearing that

purple and red salwar kameez.
Inspectors were here, she breathed

into my ear. *They say it is unsafe.*
We had all seen the cracks. Up close,

the building sounded like someone
chewing uncooked rice. And who

was surprised? Each day crews
added more floors, it seemed,

like a tower of toy blocks waiting
to topple. I am not the type

to complain. I am grateful
for work. One who cannot

read or write cannot expect
the privileges of the rich. I sew

until midnight most shifts. I sew
to feed my boys and send them

to school where I hope they learn
what they need to make

a better life. Reshma and I
hesitated. The bosses said

Don't worry, mahilaa, it's fine
and herded us through the door

like goats. *Come, come,* they said,
We have orders to fill. I turned

on my machine, a workhorse:
100 stitches per second,

so smooth it's like sewing
through ghee. If I could

afford one of my own, I would
take in jobs in our home.

It would be cramped, with all
of us in one room, but I could

roll the boys' beds during the day.
That morning, as I sat down

on my stool, I felt a shudder
and then, in a flash, the walls

were gone and the floor fell
away from my feet. I was buried

to my hips in a pile of concrete.
It took nine hours for help to come

and many more to pull me free.
But no Reshma, no Reshma,

whose name means *like silk*.
They found her two and a half

weeks later. She had survived
on rainwater and biscuits

scavenged from the rucksacks
of the dead. Even now she carries

their dust in her mouth.
Others were not as lucky.

Grandmothers, women with young
children, girls not old enough

to marry. Sweet Mita who
always bit her bottom lip

as she fed rivers of fabric
across the plate. So many lost

their lives that day. But if we
had refused to go upstairs,

we would have lost our jobs.
So we obeyed.

HR Erasure: Policy on Policy Statements

This   is   the   culture,

unwritten   for   there   are

                no   words.   The   syntax

has   been   approved.   Avoid

                pronouns   and   proper

names.   Limit   the   use

of   italics and   bold.

                Personal   information

must   be   removed.

                On   the   line   below,

write   what   you   believe

        you   have   been   told.

Recall

I cannot tell you why it took years for a safety defect to be announced.

—Mary T. Barra, CEO of General Motors, on reports that GM had evidence for a decade that ignition switches could shut off power to moving vehicles, disabling power steering, braking systems and air bags.

Tungsten Arc. That's the kind of welding
he was studying in tech school. But I always

pictured his tongue—it was longer than most.
He liked to show the girls how he could stretch it

up to touch his nose like a copperhead.
They'd say *Eww, Daddy! Ewwww!* and then:

Again! Do it again! I'll admit we were careless.
We smoked weed. We drank. Weekends the girls

stayed at our place, we left a box of Cocoa Puffs
by their mattress so they could eat in the morning

without waking us up. I won't get any awards
for step-mothering—if you can even call it that

since we weren't hitched. The day of the accident,
I was taking him to pick up his car at a buddy's house.

We'd been there the night before watching
the game. The Colts killed us, 49-14.

Like most roads in east Texas, the highway is flat—
flat as the backside of a tombstone, my granddaddy

always said. Miles of tall grass and cows grazing
behind barbed wire. The sun was sitting high up

in the sky. There was a curve. A little curve.
And that's the last I remember. I've told the story

so many times, it tells itself now. Those lawyers
dug up every bit of dirt they could find on us—

talked to his ex, to the neighbors, even tracked
down my high school teachers. It was my fault,

they said. People say something enough,
you start believing it's true. Here's all I know

for sure: when I came to, the car was smack up
against a tree, and he was laying across my lap

like he was sleeping. God knows how long
we'd been there. The blood on my arms was dry.

And I said *Baby, baby wake up. You're gonna be late
for class.* He was learning to be a welder so he could

get a job that paid better. He liked welding.
It was all about putting things back together.

Search & Rescue

I was always good at algebra—
solve for X, the teachers said.
When the levees broke,
we used X to mark the living

and the dead. We aimed
spray-paint at front doors—
or roofs, if everything else
had been swallowed—

then labeled each quadrant
with ID, date, hazards,
and bodies found. An X
on every house—that was

our goal. A decade on, I drive
around the Lower Ninth Ward
and see homes still graffitied
with my shaky orange scrawl.

Nothing to Trade

Finally we have nothing to trade, only a cough and a skeleton nobody cares about.

—from the poem "Sleepless" by Xu Lizhi, a Chinese worker who leapt to his death in September 2014 from a dormitory run by his employer, an electronics manufacturing company that produces most of the world's iPhones.

In Shenzhen, everything shines.
Mirrored windows of skyscrapers

glint like the scales of silver carp
men once caught in this seaside village.

Everything shines: silk costumes
of folk dancers who bow and twirl

for foreign tourists. The polished
marble floors of the Shajing mall,

sequined dresses of mannequins
frozen in shop displays. Imposing

gates that wall off corporate bosses'
families and luxury cars—and the sleek

sedans themselves, waxed and buffed
by drivers in dark, sparkling glasses.

Everything shines: tiny parts
on assembly lines, welding guns

that spray fireworks as if each day
is a celebration. Laminated badges

on managers who keep watch
from behind one-way glass, emerging

like birds in cuckoo clocks to bark
Faster, faster! Everything shines:

the bruised and burned limbs
of workers who earn a single break

during each 18-hour shift. The film
of chicken broth they sip standing up

before returning to their stations
early to avoid being fired or fined.

In Shenzhen, everything shines,
everything blinds.

HR Erasure: Policy on Drug and Alcohol Use

Use   alcohol   and   illegal

drugs

on   company   property

and   during

working   hours.

The   company   tolerates

impaired   workers.

You   are   under

the   influence.

You   are   under

the   influence

of   Human   Resources.

Schuhläufer

The manufacturers of the shoes tested paid the SS a fee for the 'use of prisoners.'

Sachsenhausen Concentration Camp, Oranienburg, Germany

How long will a pair of shoes last?
Days, weeks, months? The testers run

twenty-five miles a day around the track
in shoes and boots two sizes too small,

rain and wind pelting their faces and backs.
Stumble once and they are cracked

on the head with a stick. Twice and they
are loaded down with sand-filled sacks.

There are tricks to making time pass.
One man counts backwards—*hundert,*

neunundneunzig, achtundneunzig—
until his leg muscles go slack. Another

pictures his wife sitting on the banks
of the Spree, her black hair tucked under

a straw hat. Months, weeks, days, hours:
how long, how long will they last?

The Boys from Atalissa

Dozens of men with intellectual disabilities spent more than thirty years working at a turkey plant in Atalissa, Iowa, in exchange for room and board and the false promise of retirement on a ranch in Texas.

1. Willie Levi

Hang 'em doggone turkeys, boy,
they says to me. *Hang 'em good!*
And so I grabbed 'em by the legs

and yanked 'em out the coop.
Them birds was 40 pounds apiece,
'bout as much as I weighed

when I was brung on as a boy.
Talkin' turkey, that was my thing.
I'd gather up a solid wad of spit

in the back of my mouth and make
a sound like I was garglin'
salt water and bein' strangled

at the same time. And the birds
gurgled right back at me like we was
havin' a regular conversation.

I'd pat 'em on the belly and say
Okay, Tom, quiet on down now,
quiet on down, Tom, and then

when they quit their fidgetin',
I shoved 'em in the shackles
and sent 'em down to the kill room.

After that, the other boys
reached in for the livers and guts
and cut out the hearts.

'Bout 18,000 birds a day, more
'round Thanksgiving time. We was
covered in blood and when you

couldn't see no more, you stopped
to wipe your face, then did it all over
again. They say we make stuff up.

They say one of us gets to fibbin'
and the rest of us chime in like
we's repeatin' prayers at church.

But I ain't a liar. They didn't treat
us like they should. I got so used
to cockroaches droppin'

from the ceiling that even now
when I'm eatin', I cover up my food.
Hang 'em. Yes, sir. Hang 'em good.

2. Company Manual: Goals

*To teach basic vocational skills through on-the-job training
in an agricultural setting and to improve self-esteem through
a normalized work and living environment.*

3. Alford Busby

He's one of those people
you always call by their first

and last name no matter how long
you known him. Alford Busby.

Not just Alford. Not Busby.
Not Mr. Busby, that's for sure.

Alford Busby. He weren't afraid
to say no. *Alford Busby,* they say

to him, *go on to bed. Alford Busby,
turn off that TV.* Alford Busby

says *I ain't goin' to bed. Ima sit
right here and watch* Gunsmoke.

And Alford Busby would sit
on that itchy plaid sofa and plant

his feet on the floor so hard
the rats would go running

off to every corner of the room.
They says *Alright then,*

*Alford Busby, get your hands up
on the pole,* and they'd pull him

up by his big ol' arms
and make him hold that pole

for hours and hours. We'd eat
dinner and wash the dishes

and Alford Busby would still
be holdin' that pole like he was

keepin' the bunkhouse
from fallin' down on our heads.

One day it got to snowin' hard.
They tells Alford Busby *Time for bed,*

boy, and he gets mad, so mad.
Alford Busby says *That's it,*

and he walks out the door—
this was before they put the chains

on. He walks out in the snow
until he's gone. They looked

for him but Alford Busby
weren't nowhere

to be found. We whispered
'bout where he went, 'bout how

he musta made it to the ranch
they promised us we'd move to

when we retired. It has horses
runnin' free and a pond packed

so full of fish that your rod
never comes up empty.

They even say we can have
a dog, and I have in mind a sheltie

like the one I had back home
before I was sent away. Mitzi.

She liked to lick my face after I ate
buttered corn. It was spring

when they found Alford Busby.
Things was startin' to thaw

and a farmer on Wiggins Road
found him face down in his field

frozen solid, no boots
or coat. They made sure we

knowed about it, said *Don't you
be gettin' no ideas o' your own.*

We was all sad. Alford Busby
was 37 years old. Alford Busby

weren't afraid to say no.
Alford Busby was our hero.

4. Company Manual: Retention

*For most clients, a good adjustment is made and this is reflected
in the record of a low 15 percent turnover rate.*

5. Mrs. Avery

We called them *The Boys* even though
they were grown men, some older

than we were. They always seemed happy.
They came to the parades and town fair.
Those boys loved the dunking booth.
Harold Miner always made sure each of them
hit the target. How they'd laugh and laugh
when the platform collapsed and the bank president
or school principal went down with a splash!

They attended Sunday school, and even though
some of the hymns were a mouthful for them,
they hummed along as best they could.
We'd see them in the Mini-Mart counting out
pennies for honey buns and a cold pop,
and if they were short a nickel or a dime,
one of us would always slide a coin across
the counter. I mean, I'm sure the labor was hard,

but they seemed proud to earn their keep,
and what were the options, really, for the mentally re–,
mentally challenged? In the early days, they'd have
Christmas parties and open houses, and we would
sip punch and admire the evergreen garlands
they'd strung in the dining room. Back then,
they had a pool table and a gym and caretakers
who seemed nice. One of the boys could tap
out Jingle Bells with a plastic fork and spoon.

How were we to know things had gotten so bad?
When I read in the *Muscatine Journal* about
the rodents and mold, I said to my husband,
If you look up the word deplorable *in the dictionary,
this is what you'll find.* We felt sick with shame.
We called them *The Boys* and sometimes even
Our Boys. I want the world to know that we are
not to blame.

6. Company Manual: Recognition

For his innovative work with mentally retarded men, company co-founder T.H. Johnson received the coveted 'Employer of the Year' award from the National Association for Retarded Citizens.

7. Denise Gonzales

I thought I'd seen everything
a social worker could see:
children sleeping in dog crates,
seniors with bed sores the size

of saucers. But nothing could
prepare me for what I found
in that old schoolhouse: 21 men
with rotting teeth, toenails

so long they curled into the pads
of their feet like leeches.
And the smell: urine-soaked
mattresses, mouse feces, bodies

that hadn't been bathed
in weeks. Their forked hands
were covered in what looked like
a bad rash. We learned it was

dried blood. Turkey blood.
Yet still they reached out
to welcome me. *You the new
boss lady?* they asked.

8. Company Manual: Costs

Average client monthly income: $750.
Average client monthly expenses: $750.

9. Keith Brown

Some o' the others is in nursin' homes
now. Bobby and Billy Penner live
on their own up to Waterloo.

Ron and Johnny moved back
with family. Pete and Doyle is gone.
I got me an apartment in Arkansas.

I got a job and a cat. I like to watch
The Price is Right. I like the part
when they spin that big wheel.

I never miss a day of work. I never
eat no turkey. I never hurt another
bird 'cause I know how it feels.

HR Erasure: Policy on Illness or Injury

In   your   illness

     human   nature   may

        reduce   you

to   questions.

        You   are   sick.

    You   are   lost.

You   use   all   of

        your   time   off.

    You   use   all   of

        your   time.

You   may   be   granted

        a   leave   of

    absence   from   life.

Indigo

I'm training the new girl just in
from down river. She comes clutching
a flour sack her momma stuffed

with all her worldlies: a whittled spoon
and a rag baby made of cotton scraps,
the smile drawn on with a pencil.

When she asks how to call me, I say Indigo,
though it's not my given name, to tell
the truth. Indigo like the flower we grow

in the fields. Indigo 'cause the Master's boy
looked at me one day and said to Missus,
"Mama, her skin's so black it's blue."

Sophie, Louisa, Josephine, Polly, Rosille, Philis, Lucie.

Her name is Cecilia, says call her Cilly.
She's to help me with the cooking
in the kitchen out back. I show her

how to hang a pig from hooks
in the rafters, how to chop little wheels
of okra on the block, how to keep the fire

going under the pots. Six meals a day
for 300 souls, three a day for the house,
another three for the rest of us.

Feliciana, Magdalaine, Clara, Angelica, Pauline, Esnée, Celeste.

July hits you like a big old wall of heat
and the cook fires make it hotter still,
like taking a bath in a sugar kettle.

Cilly about near faints her first day,
so I teach her my trick: tie a wet cloth
'round your neck.

Isabelle, Marinette, Rose, Florestan, Philomene, Felicite, Claire.

The Missus has one job: to make
sure we do ours. She watches us
from the doorjamb, wiping

her soft hands down the side of her skirts
like they need cleaning. Always fix
the trays of food in the side pantry

before serving, I explain to Cilly.
The staging area, Missus calls it.
Nobody wants to see how it got done.

Etienne, Hortense, Honoré, Fanny, Dosse, Cloé, Adelaide.

I teach her how to keep the cold goods cold
in the olive jar and how to snip sugar.
Missus takes one snip—Master, he likes two.

I show her how to pour the wine
and rum and then stand aside
till they motion for more. Your feet get

weary-tired on the brick floor, but we can't
have rugs on account of the flooding.
The Mississippi gives no warning

before it pays a visit—we've got to haul
the table and chairs upstairs
when waters start licking at the doors.

Clementine, Delphine, Betsie, Marianne, Noel, Caroline, Zepherine.

Cooking beats churning the sugar,
I tell Cilly—that's round-the-clock work.
Barattez, barattez, barattez!

Nights you see candles winking
and hear the paddles scraping against
copper kettles, the wind whipping

palm fronds, men groaning when sugar
leaps up like foam from a mad dog,
burning them on the arms and face.

Ebram, Jacob, Andre, Bellick, Thomas, Lucien, Norbert.

I catch Cilly staring at the parlor ceiling
painted fancy by that artist from Italy.
He took sick and the Missus let him stay,

so he repaid her with more pictures.
The man, he talked funny, but the Missus,
she giggled at every word that came

out of his mouth. "Those pictures
aren't for your eyes," I tell Cilly.
"Your eyes belong on the ground."

I say, "You look up and they'll think
you're trying to be like God above—
or worse, like them."

Elvina, Virginia, Eliza, Nelly, Charlotte, Jenny, Rosella.

One of these days I'll tell her about Sarah,
the girl with teeth so white and pretty,
like a string a shimmery pearls. The Missus

caught her smiling wide in a china plate
admiring all those shiny teeth smiling back.
The Missus won't have that.

Next thing we know the caretaker
drags Sarah down to the blacksmith shop,
lays her head on the anvil,

and knocks her perfect pearls out
one by one. Poor girl's got a mouthful
of darkness now.

Marie, Patrice, Coralie, Dorothy, Lise, Rose, Erasie.

I show her how to warm the sheets
with a coal pan, how to slide it under
the covers real slow. Don't warm Master's bed

with your own self, I warn, but I can't tell
if she hears me right. She's young
but not too young—this much I know.

A man named Living. A woman named Time.
A girl named Girl. A boy named Son.
And me, Indigo. Indigo trade. Indigo dye.

Nobody wants to see how it got done.

II

Raise the Rent

Someone evidently got the idea of having a few friends in as paying party guests a few days before the landlord's scheduled monthly visit .... Thus was the Harlem rent-party born.

—Frank Boyd, *American Life Histories: Manuscripts from the Federal Writers' Project, 1936-1940*

Like Miss Bessie sang: *On my door*
they nailed a sign, I got to move from here
if the rent man don't change his mind.

So fill up the bathtub with firewater,
slide the sofa against the wall, hoist a piano
from the street below with a rope

and a prayer. Stack the mattresses,
switch the light bulbs for yellow and blue,
and cook up a pile of food: chicken and fish,

pork chops, gumbo, collard greens, sweets.
Call Dusty Fletcher and Stump & Stumpy
to get us stomping on the wood floors—

and be sure to invite the neighbors so they
don't get sore from all the noise. We need
a doorman to collect a quarter a head,

and if they want to eat, it's 10 cents more.
Cheaper than a club—funkier, too,
especially when the lights go low

and you grab the closest girl and do
the mess-around and the slow drag.
We got sailors from the ports, domestics,

workers coming off late factory shifts.
The handbill says it all: *You don't*
get nothing for being an angel, child,

so you might as well get real busy
and real wild. Call it a shindig, scuffle,
struggle, shake-me-down, chitterling rag.

Give the drummer a blanket to muffle
his traps—we don't need more police uptown.
We're gonna dance and drink and sing

till the sun peeks through the tenements,
a little wink of orange you see when you
stagger downstairs. You yawn and stretch

and count your loot on the stoop out front.
If you're lucky, you just bought yourself
a mild bust-head and another month.

Ike Turner's Obituary

Tina

Tina
Tina

Tina
Tina

Tina

Tina
Tina

Tina

Tina

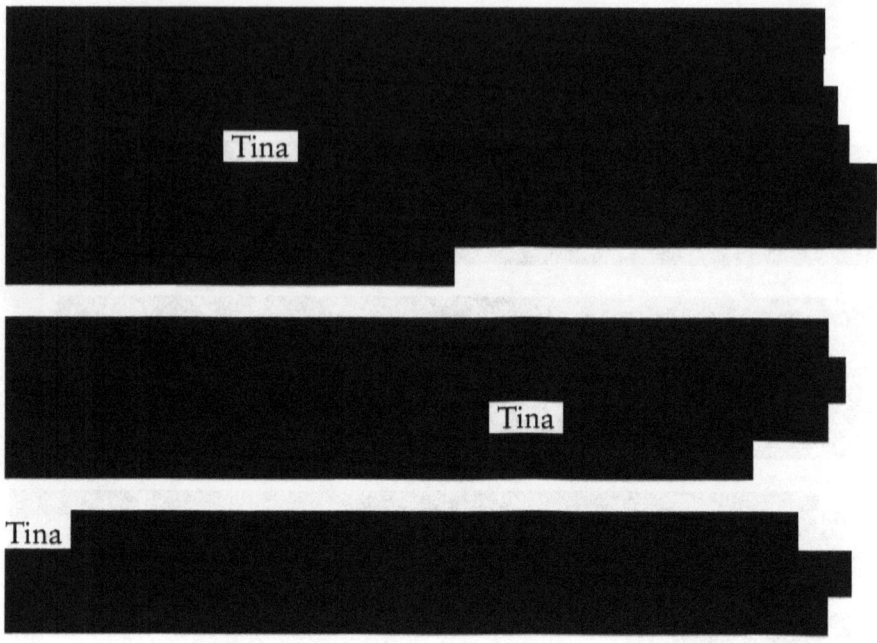

Man Walks 21 Miles to Work and Back

I can spend a mile or more on the sound
my boots make in the snow. People say

crunch, but it's closer to *church*,
like when my momma used to say,

*Get your backside outta bed, son—it's time
for church.* That was the beat of her walk

through life: *church, church, church.*
Faith, faith, faith. Me, I hear the legends,

how Bo Diddley found an open chord on a guitar
and rapped it like a drum: *Shave and a haircut,*

two bits. Or the way a banjo player frails & knocks,
downstroking to a rhythm all his own.

That's what I hear when I march from 8 Mile
to the M-59: *right foot, left foot, right.*

Got mugged one summer in Highland Park.
Couple of young kids. They didn't get much,

just a watch and a few bucks. Roughed me up
some. But mostly folks just pass me by.

Cars in the rain got a certain sound—
they go *wish, wish, wish.*

Gary at the Auto Glass Plant

Out on the line, the machines are so loud
he hears them in his teeth, no matter how deep
he shoves rubber plugs in his ears. Camaraderie
comes in high-fives and nods. He can work

a year without learning a guy's name. Not that
he'd hear it now anyway, even with a proper
introduction. Being half-deaf has its advantages,
though. When his daughter moves back home

with a colicky baby, he can't hear his grandson
crying. Later, building castles at the beach,
he can't hear him ask *Grandpa, is glass
really made out of sand?* His wife jokes

he never listened to her before, either,
but they both know that's not true. He always
asked about her day in the junior high office,
laughed about the excuses some kids had

for missing school, like the boy who got
sprayed by a skunk and the girl who was
allergic to chalk. He likes when strangers ask
the time because they point to their wrists

as a clue and he can trot out an old favorite:
Time for you to get a watch, bud,
before adding *Just joking—it's half-past three.*
Most of the time he feels like he's living

inside a world of glass—a 6 millimeter-thick
shatterproof dome laminated with PVB.
There's half the employees and twice the work
at the plant these days. They barely get used

to one owner before he up and sells to another.
New rules, new signs, tanned guys in ties
coming through with clipboards and ideas,
acting like they've worn a hardhat before.

Last month management started timing
bathroom breaks. You get six minutes a shift,
including the time it takes to clock in and out.
First comes a warning, then a suspension,

then you're cleaning out your locker.
If you don't go at all, you earn a $1 gift card
per day. Gary suspects the young ones
with their steel bladders will rack up

the rewards. Most of the old guys don't stand
a chance—they'll piss their way to a pink slip
before the next payday. They'll linger
in the parking lot taking the last drag

off a cigarette before peeling off for good.
But not Gary. No sir, not him. If there's
one thing he's learned after all these years,
it's how to hold it in.

Econ Textbook Erasure

The   price

of   happiness

      is   shame.   Our   organs

   are   outsourced.   We   ration

      promises,   justify   our

lust,   default   on   our

      souls.   Cola   soap

cigars   water   lattes

      TVs   guns.

      What   is   the   cost

      of   a   bulletproof

            mood?   The   market

knows.   This   is

            America   101.

If You Are a Massage Therapist in a Seasonal Town

you'd better carry a concealed weapon.
There are men who want you to rub their
backs. There are men who want you.
There are men who want. There are men
who slip the sheets off ample bellies,
fumble for their flimsiest parts. If you are
a massage therapist in a seasonal town
where tourists blow in and out like ocean wind,
you learn new anatomical terms: *Put your junk
away*, you tell the businessman, the pilot,

the pastor of a southern congregation who grabs
your hand and commands you to pray.
The pistol at your hip is stiffer than any dick.
You could have finished nursing school.
You could have enlisted like your sister.
You are a massage therapist in a seasonal town.
There are men who want you like a child
wants a souvenir. There are men who want.
There are men. There are. *There, there.*
There are no happy endings here.

Trailer Parks 101

a seminar on the art of buying and operating mobile home communities

Whatever you do, do not include water. I swear, some folks will leave the tap on all day and night just because they can. They will run you dry—literally. And no laundry rooms—tree roots wreak havoc on the sewer lines. You'll have yourself a plumber on speed dial before you can say *spin cycle*. As far as rents go, $495 is the magic number, the sweet spot. $500 is the kiss of death. But here's a secret: you can bump up land rent—or *dirt rent*, as the tenants call it—10 percent a year with nary a complaint. A few extra bucks a month is nothing compared to the 3K it'll cost them to haul a trailer to a new lot, not to mention deposits. Phone and cable companies raise their rates each year, so it's almost expected. Besides, where we used to get mostly seniors on fixed incomes, now we've got two or more workers in a household. They can always pick up another shift or two at Burger King. My business partner—nowadays, I have to say *business partner* because he's not *that* kind of partner, if you get my drift— though you get that type, too, so I don't judge. And you know what? They keep their properties neat, flowers everywhere. Anyway, we have 130 parks in 18 states. Our investors double their money every four years. We are a no-frills operation. If there's a swimming pool, we fill it in. We get rid of the vending machines and game rooms. We don't lure people in with fancy brochures and clubhouses. Some people will tell you to always say *homes*, not *trailers*. *Homes*. But I say if it quacks like a duck, it's a duck. Why sugarcoat it? Frankly, *mobile home* is not much better. The only mobility most of these folks have is downward. That said, it doesn't hurt to give your park a name that suggests a vacation or resort: Holiday Manor or Lakeside Estates, even if there's no body of water for miles. People like living somewhere that sounds classy. And believe it or not, some residents are here by choice. I had a lady down near Waco who ordered so much stuff off QVC that she rented a second trailer to store it all. She could have opened her own store with all the junk she bought. But you've got your share of deadbeats, too. I recommend a strict

No pay, no stay policy. It sounds cold, but you aren't doing them any favors by delaying the inevitable. Now let's talk about you. Maybe you're worried about retirement. Maybe your job's about to be outsourced to India or a country ending in *stan* where some guy who can't speak English is supposed to talk you through rebooting your laptop. Please. Don't get me started. Anyway, you're looking at the right time. With all the foreclosures, people need a roof over their heads. Doesn't have to be a pretty roof, as you can see. We're not talking French Champagne—at best, it's cheap beer. Like I always say, just keep telling yourself *It's not like I'm going to be living here.*

McRant

Mike thinks he's all that 'cause he wears
a blue dress shirt and tie. I want to get right up
in his greasy face and say *You're nothing
but a McManager—get over yourself.*
But that'll land me on drive-thru duty all winter,
the fast-food version of solitary confinement—
four hours in the freezing cold. Sure, they give you
a jacket, but it's so thin you can see through it.
Oh, and don't forget the fingerless gloves—
by the end of the shift, your fingertips
are so numb you could dip 'em in the deep fryer
and not feel the pain. Meanwhile, Mike yells
at us over every little thing: *I need more nuggets,
STAT!* he screams like he's a surgeon
saving lives. Of course he's sweet as pie
to the customers. This one lady spent
10 minutes making me describe every salad
in great detail, then ordered a chicken sandwich.
When I counted out her change, she wrinkled
up her face. *This nickel is dirty,* she says to me.
Dirty! Like every other coin she's ever touched
was sanitized and individually wrapped.
I want a clean nickel, she tells me. Well, I already
closed the register, so I have to get Mike to come over
and key in his secret override number that he protects
like it's the launch code for a nuclear bomb.
And do you know what he tells her? He says
*Oh yes, ma'am, you're right—that nickel is filthy.
Let's get you a new one,* and he digs around until he
finds the shiniest coin in the drawer. The lady
walks away and Mike turns to me with his supersized
sneer and says *Krista, do not let that happen again.*
I want to say *It's Trista, McAsshat. The least you
could do is learn my name.*

HR Erasure: Policy on Manager Responsibilities

Violate your country

and principles

every day.

Learn that no one

expects you to be

good. Business must

always come first.

Avoid the appearance

of ethics.

Make sure

everyone gets hurt.

Senate Bill 730, 1893

Be it enacted that the first
Monday of September
in each year, the day
celebrated and known
as Labor's Holiday,
is hereby made a legal
public day to save

on washers and dryers
and jewelry and tools,
to save save save on sofas
and bedding and guns
and shoes, save save save
until we have everything
left to lose.

Sonntagsleerung

the depression one feels on Sunday before the workweek begins

A bee with a crimped wing
scales each blade of grass
in your backyard, inching
his way to the tip before

toppling on the sod cubicle
where he flails and spins
then tries again. The lawn
is an inbox of urgent green.

Maybe this fringed bit, or this,
will give him the needed lift.
Such an optimistic little
Sisyphus. *Insolvent* doesn't

mean what it should mean.
You wish he could just quit.

Billable Minutes

All the minutes spent conjuring
names for rock bands that will

never exist: *Blue Genes,*
You Can't Lick Your Elbow.

Or the time spent wondering
why we say *inadvertent* but not

advertent—as in *I advertently*
kicked him in the balls—and why

things *unfurl* but rarely *furl*, unless
you count the Miracle Fortune Fish,

its whisper of red plastic curling
in your palm. Slip the fish from its

wax-paper sleeve, close your eyes,
and wish for all the money in the world,

for all the money in the world
to melt like cotton candy at a carnival.

Vultures

There is one and only one social responsibility of business—to use its resources and engage in activities designed to increase its profits.

—Milton Friedman

Today when I came home, all the garbage
in the neighborhood was smeared across
the street and lawns. Buzzards, my husband said.

The bones from our barbecue ribs
looked like they'd been steam-cleaned.
Even the cat litter had been picked through,

nothing left but clumps of dust. This week
Whole Foods announced it's cutting benefits
for 1,900 part-time workers *to better meet*

the needs of our business. Turkey buzzards
on the side of the road look like men in dark suits
hunched over the latest financial statements

in a board room. When I pass them on my
morning walks, they don't even startle.
Whole Foods was recently bought by

Amazon owner Jeff Bezos. I read that this cut
will save the company the amount Bezos earns
in six hours. I frequently mistake soaring

buzzards for eagles. Scavenger or sacred symbol—
why scorn one and not the other? Who belongs
behind bars? Who should grace the Forbes cover?

A birder friend told me the flight feathers
of a buzzard are lighter underneath than its body
and wingbone. *Look for the sign of the cross,*

she explained. *Let the market decide,* economists
always say. In the end, it doesn't matter.
A bird of prey is a bird of prey.

The Swimmers and the CEOs

Drowning doesn't look like drowning.
It's surprisingly quiet, almost serene.

Victims seem to be climbing invisible
ladders. They can't cry or scream.

So many swimmers, heads bobbing,
arms struggling to break the surface.

They can barely keep afloat.
Meanwhile, the dry folks on shore

glance up from shiny magazines.
Oh look, they say, *They're waving to us.*

And so they smile and wave back
to the little people in the sea.

Panama Papers Erasure

The word yacht appears in the documents 19,380 times.

—*New York Times, May 29, 2016*

yacht   yacht   yacht

yacht   yacht   yacht   yacht

yacht   yacht   yacht

yacht   yacht

yacht   yacht   yacht

yacht   yacht

yacht

yacht

yacht   yacht   yacht   yacht

yacht   yacht   yacht   yacht

yacht   yacht

yacht   yacht

yacht   yacht   yacht

yacht

yacht   yacht   yacht   yacht

yacht   yacht   yacht

          yacht   yacht   yacht

yacht   yacht   yacht   yacht...

You Break It, You Bought It: A Villain-elle
January 2025

Our nation's fate is a retail rule—
You break it, you bought it.
But the metaphor is broken, too.

They is what we mean by *you*.
It's the *it* that's slippery as a fish.
Our nation's fate is a retail rule.

Is the *it* the country they overthrew
or the people, splintered and split?
The metaphor is broken, too.

Capitol, capital—a free market coup,
human rights sold to the highest bid.
Our nation's fate is a retail rule.

A poet said it so it must be true:
The record keepers are the poets.
Unless the metaphor is broken, too.

When it's life & death, not *Family Feud*,
who'll be left to write the obit?
Our nation's fate is a retail rule.
The metaphor is broken, too.

In Human Resources

In Human Resources
the weather is always

fluorescent. There are no
flies, only files in Human

Resources. The plastic
ficus plant wilts

in Human Resources.
In Human Resources

the motivational poster
of Mount Everest

tilts to the right.
In Human Resources,

in Human Resources,
in Human Resources.

In Human Resources
a calendar on the wall

has no months or dates.
Do not bother to smile

for your photo ID
in Human Resources.

In Human Resources
no one has a face.

III

Shitshow

Shitshow should be one word
       is a thought I've had at least

three times this week. Not
       shit [stop] show as the dictionaries

and Autocorrect insist. What
       do they know? Shit is not modifying

show—it is the show and the show
       is shit: tarry dung, inexorable

excrement. Yesterday, for example,
       we saw an elderly man try to exit—

I know, I know *disembark*—
       a luxury sailboat. Unhinged on one side,

the sliver of dock became,
       with each step, a horizontal seesaw,

the already unsteady man teetering
       left right left. Those of us sipping

margaritas at the nearby tiki bar
       gasped but didn't help. Collectively,

we did that thing where you faux lunge
       with no intention of actually budging.

Sure, class was at play—a man
       with a toy worth more than the homes

some of us were lucky enough
        to almost own. *Not it, not it.*

Who among us didn't secretly want
        to see this Thurston Howell III pitch

into the brackish bay below? Which
        of us was the show, which the shit?

What Did You Do Last Week?

1. I lay in bed and thought of the AA mantra
   one day at a time and the Dolly Parton lyric
   I've had to think up a way to survive
   and the Becket line *I can't go on. I'll go on.*

2. I scattered a few bucks like birdseed
   to causes I care about.

3. I sat in meetings where there were calls
   to order and motions on motions,
   oceans of motions. Someone in the shadows
   was always taking minutes. *Taking minutes.*

4. I went for a walk in a wetland preserve
   nestled between an asphalt company
   and the county courthouse. A northern flicker
   pecked for ground beetles. On its head:
   a red brushstroke like an artist's
   afterthought. Or a warning. I wondered
   if birds have blood. I wondered if the people
   in power have feelings. I wondered
   if we'll go on. I told myself we can't
   not go on.

5. I wrote this poem.

Elegy for the 30-Year Career

My mother's father, raised on a farm,
spent his working years at a helicopter plant.
He rose at 4 a.m., left home by 5 sharp.
His lunchbox looked like a metal barn.

Inside: two turkey sandwiches on rye
slathered with cranberry sauce,
a banana, and a Thermos of black coffee,
all packed by my grandmother

when she returned from second shift
at the factory. For thirty years
he drove back roads from Pascoag
across the Connecticut state line.

He had heart bypass surgery in his fifties
to fix the disease that killed
his twin. Insurance kicked in, nothing
out of pocket. He had three weeks'

paid vacation. One spring he used
his time off to build the wishing well
my grandmother had always wanted.
Most summers they visited us down South,

their silver Airstream camper a sideways
silo in front of our house. When he retired,
he had a pension, benefits, and more time
to watch *Judge Judy* and help motorists

who were stranded or lost. And when he died,
he left his wife a house, some savings,
and the memory of a man who never had
a bad word for his company or his boss.

The Doorkeepers

I live across the street
from a junior high school
in western Pennsylvania.
When it snows—and it snows

all winter long—the district's
maintenance workers arrive
with shovels and blowers
and plows, scraping, dumping

and *beep-beeping* in reverse
under my bedroom window.
In bad storms they start
at midnight and work

till dawn, the sidewalks
cleared just before
the groan of school buses.
Sometimes, though, the snow

is relentless, and by 6 a.m.
I hear the equipment yawn
to a halt. All goes silent.
Soon the superintendent

will send a recorded
phone message announcing
a cancellation or delay.
By February, his voice is

a weary sigh: *Good morning,
parents* .... And you know
he's thinking *If this keeps up,
we'll be here till July.*

Where do the workers go?
Back to bed? Or off
to keep the ancient boiler
purring like a tamed lion?

Once when my son was
in 8th grade, a local attorney
was a no-show for career day.
The principal replaced him

with the longtime janitor.
He wore his blue jumpsuit,
my son said. I picture his
name on the chest—*Ray*

or *Ed*—but that's likely
my own embellishment.
Even a 13-year-old boy
cringed at the questions:

What level of education
prepared you for your job?
What do you like best
about the path you chose?

The janitor answered
as seriously as the banker
and the pediatrician.
What I like best, he said,

is being alone in the building
at the end of the day. I turn
my radio up as loud as I want.
Some evenings when I

draw the blinds, I see him
framed in the yellow glow
of a classroom. He's stacking
desks to mop the floors—

night after night, year
after year, moving
to the sound of a song
I can't quite hear.

End of the Season

This beach town was our first
getaway as a couple

thirty years ago. We barely
left the room for three days,

surfacing only to share a pizza
or antipasto and a pitcher of beer

at Grotto's. That's when you
could get an oceanfront room

for $60 instead of $600. Tonight
Lower Case Blues will play

at The Pond, and the bearded
bass guitarist will wear sunglasses

during every set. Last night
was the bartender's birthday,

and now one of the high-tops
is reserved for his picked-over cake.

This year-round place used to be
called The Frog Pond and was

a popular lesbian bar. One night
when a friend's band was playing,

our then 4-year-old son stationed
himself at the mini-basketball game

in the corner. Patrons gathered
to cheer him on, taking turns

ponying up a dollar for the next
set of balls. Balls—there were

lots of jokes about balls. I'm not sure
when it transitioned to a mainly

hetero joint or when they dropped
the "Frog." It makes me think

of my favorite dress made by
a company called Horny Toad

that changed its name to the more
generic Toad & Co., distancing itself,

I assume, from internet search results
triggered by *horny*. That change makes

some sense. The Pond—not so much.
Now it feels like any other bar

broadcasting the Eagles game
on twenty TVs. At lunch this afternoon,

our waiter was from Romania.
He's about our son's age, mid-20s,

here on a seasonal work visa.
Tedy brought his own bottle

of prune brandy—*truica*—
to last him the summer in the States,

and now, as the last of the tourists
trickle through town, he is down

to the dregs. His father named him
for Teddy Roosevelt and swears

he spelled it three times
for the hospital nurse in Timișoara

who nevertheless put just one "d"
on the birth certificate. Yesterday

was Meterless Monday, the first
off-season day when parking

is free. Bikes are allowed
on the boardwalk again, and early

in the morning it's like
the Tour de France between Spring Lake

and Henlopen Acres, with cyclists
in neon Spandex zooming by

in packs. Our son learned to ride
a two-wheeler on this boardwalk

the spring he turned five. He only
fell once near Funland. This is

the time of year when most businesses
are shuttering, a word that always

makes me think of *shuddering*,
which we'll be doing soon enough, too.

Thrasher's has closed one of its two
French fry stands and now cashiers

don't have to spend as much time
explaining why there's no ketchup—

salt & vinegar, a tradition since 1929.
Dolle's orange script saltwater taffy sign

reminds me of my mother writing daily
to our daughter at her first sleepaway camp.

What did the letters say? I asked.
I have no idea, she shrugged.

They were written in cursive.
My friend Roselyn sent me a meme

last week: *Someday us old folks
will use cursive as a secret code.*

On this foggy day, the ocean
and sky merged at the seam.

I read that something like this
caused JFK, Jr.'s plane crash

off the coast of Martha's Vineyard
—he may have been unable

to tell which way was up.
Spatial disorientation, they call it.

There are a lot of references
to U.S. presidents in this poem,

presidents who—while not
perfect—seemed like they were

trying to steer our country
away—not toward—darkness.

They are ghosts now, like so many
landmarks that have closed.

We say *Turn left at the old
Stoney Lonen* or *It's right across from*

where Lingo's Market used to be.
We walk past the Oceanus Motel

and remember when the pool
had a diving board. Our daughter

counted the days till she turned six—
the minimum age for diving—

only to arrive that summer
crushed to discover the board

had been removed. Liability
issues, the manager said.

When your children grow up
and leave home, everything

is a ghost landmark. Every memory
can make you half laugh, half cry.

The horizon is a blue blur. It's hard
to tell sky from sea, sea from sky.

Street Sweeper in the Key of E

The truck groans up the block.
Sprayers splash, bristles spin.

Women in bathrobes, men in plaid
boxers dash out doors to shoehorn

cars into spaces across the street.
Last night's windstorm knocked

tangled branches in its path.
From my kitchen, I see the driver

pause as if willing the debris
to disappear. Or perhaps

he'd rather churn it to mulch
under the eight-ton weight

of his tires. Instead, he shoves
his hands into heavy-duty yellow

gloves and climbs out of the cab.
One by one he feeds the limbs

into a secret hatch, then hoists
himself behind the wheel,

captain of a landlocked
boat. I am the street sweeper.

You are the street sweeper.
The truck hums its only note.

The Egg Inspector

travels from market to market,
parking on the side where stock boys

smoke between shifts. In the dairy aisle,
he wields a clipboard and favorite pen:

an ultra-fine black retractable gel.
He has a favorite egg brand, too,

but he won't tell—it would be unethical.
He pries open the cartons, checks

to make sure each egg is intact,
then looks for specks and cracks,

places where the membrane is so thin
the yolk peeks through like a tiny sun.

He and his wife can't have children.
The fertility specialist waved a wand

over her ovaries and said the problem
was not quantity but quality. He knows

a good egg when he sees one.
Most are good, so he checks the box

that says *pass. Pass, pass, pass.*
Some are *missing* or *flawed.* If a batch

seems tainted, he checks *adulterated.*
He hates that word. It makes him blush.

The dairy manager at the Fresh & Fast
in Scranton makes him blush, too.

She wears a white lab coat like a doctor.
Underneath, her shirts outline breasts

that are just the right size. *Look at her
eyes*, he reminds himself. *Pass, pass, pass.*

He thinks of his wife worrying over
crossword puzzles. He thinks of his wife

whisking batter for lemon pound cake.
He understands how fragile some things

can be. You must cup them in your hands
so they don't break.

HR Erasure: Policy on the Birth of a Child

You are normal
normal up until
the day
the baby is born.
The day the baby
is born
you change. You are
a mother mother
mother. You are
a mother
mother mother as
long as you are
normal normal.
If not, you may
want to revise
your life. You may
want to change your

child.   Employees   must   be

        transparent   in   their   needs.

        You   have   the   option

of   being   relieved.

Transactions

When was the last time you counted out change,
the last time you felt a cash register drawer spring open

against your belly, cracked a roll of quarters, licked
your thumb to separate wrinkled bills? I worked

at an ice cream parlor after school. A widower came
every Wednesday, ordered butter pecan in a dish.

He asked about my classes, told me stories about
his dead wife. When he mentioned his diagnosis,

I was too young to know the difference between
prostate and *prostrate*. I mumbled *Sorry* and slid

the coins across the speckled Formica. I remember
the first time I paid for something on my own.

My friend Shana and I went to the diner of the motor inn
where our families were staying near Hershey Park.

She was 7, I was 5. We had pancakes and chocolate milk.
When the bill came, we emptied our pockets, counted

the exact amount. Shana said, *We need to leave a tip*.
So we left a penny, which seemed like enough. This must

have been right around when Shana's stepfather started creeping
into her bedroom at night in exchange for a stuffed pony,

then a stereo, and later, a cherry red Camaro with flames
on the hood. That morning at breakfast, Shana felt guilty

about not ordering orange juice. *My mom says
I need vitamin C or I'll get scurvy.* After we paid she said,

*Let's go back to the room and wash our hands.
My mom says money's dirty.*

Midterm

This is the point in the semester
when college girls cry softly

in bathroom stalls, flushing
to mask the sobs, then exit to check

their mascara in mirrors. Maybe
it's a rough exam or papers

piling up like laundry. Most likely,
it's a boy—a high school love

who's found someone else. Or
it's a new crush who won't

return her texts. A decade ago
I had a first-year nursing student

in freshman comp. She made
straight As, never missed a class.

In mid-October, she disappeared
for two weeks. When she came

to my office, she could only heave,
each syllable catching in her chest.

She had returned to Pittsburgh
for the weekend and broken up

with her longtime boyfriend.
It was a difficult decision.

His family was her family.
His mother taught her to make

potato and cheese pierogies.
But things had changed.

Or she had changed. He took it
better than she had expected.

The next day, he hanged himself.
I did what I could do: gave her

hugs and tissues, walked her
to the counseling center. This is

the point in the semester
when college girls cry softly

in bathroom stalls. We meet
at the row of sinks where I wash

my hands, pluck a gray hair.
The girls blow their noses, dab

their tears. They cannot know
yet the difference between pain

that lasts a matter of days
and the weight we carry for years.

Unlucky

My son's varsity soccer teammate
worked after school at the local
Subway sandwich shop. One day

he opened the alley door
to take out the garbage, and a man
shot him in the face. It was April 2009.

Minimum wage was $7.15 an hour,
a paltry amount that somehow
compounds the loss. I can look up

that figure on the internet, but I can't
Google my son's reaction when I told him
Scott had died. Or maybe

he told me, news in high school
traveling at the speed of the bullet
that killed him. Or the bullet

that lodged in his co-worker's hip.
Or the bullet that killed the man
who was checking his mail

when the shooter was trying to escape.
I can't search for the feeling that settled
over our small town like pre-dawn fog.

And there's no record of the words
I offered his parents at the funeral
or, six months later, when we shared a table

at the soccer banquet, boys shuffling
to the podium to accept plaques
for *most improved* and MVP. I do recall

that we sat with the school principal
who asked what I taught. *English,* I said.
My least favorite subject, she groaned,

adding that she treats punctuation
like Christmas ornaments, sprinkling
a comma here, an apostrophe there.

The team's British coach had a stock response
when players lost possession or missed a goal.
Unlucky! he'd shout from the sidelines,

shorthand for *It's not your fault.*
With his accent, it sounded more like *unlooky,*
and we parents started saying it ourselves

for every bad call or botched pass
as we sat bundled up on the bleachers,
the last of the sunlight dipping below

the Alleghenies. The man who shot Scott
had served three tours of duty in Iraq.
PTSD, the papers said. He wasn't supposed

to have a gun. He'd had a fight with his wife
at a bowling alley before he stormed across
Plank Road to the sandwich shop. During

the trial, a mother of a veteran invited
his wife to Thanksgiving dinner. *I understand,*
she wrote. She'd lost her own son

to suicide. The shooter was convicted. Yes,
he was the shooter, but I should say he was also
a veteran, a husband, a father, a son.

In a blog, there's a picture of him holding
his daughter. She's wearing red and white
snowflake pajamas. Her arms are looped

around his neck. Last month—ten years
after the shooting—he killed himself in prison.
Self-inflicted laceration, they said on the news.

When you search online, you find
another soldier with the same name
who received a posthumous Silver Star.

Scott was a senior. He planned to study
electronic technology at a nearby
community college. He wouldn't get

to drive his Pontiac Sunbird
to campus, blasting heavy metal
on Route 22. He wouldn't pass

the McDonald's and remember teasing
the coach for the way he pronounced it—
Mac-Done-ald's—when they stopped

for burgers after away games.
He wouldn't sit in the alumni section
for the district championship

the following season. And when
they won—defeating their biggest rival
in double overtime—he wouldn't be there

to take part in our town's ritual:
greeting the returning players
with blaring car horns as police cruisers

and fire trucks guided the bus back to school,
sirens shrieking. Wary residents peered
through front doors fearing the worst

when they heard the noise, then waved,
relieved to see that this time we were
celebrating one of life's small, loaded joys.

HR Erasure: Policy on Clarity

Use   euphemisms.

        Be   ambiguous.

Choose   your   own   definitions

            for   words,

your   own   geography

      of   jargon.   Rightsize

          your   reality.

The   company   adjusts.

          The   company

             seeks   feedback.

The   company   empowers.

      All   days   are   not

    days.   All   hours

are   not   hours.   All   hours

    are   not   ours.

Call It a Bone

First you tie a fist
full of pine needles
into a knot, twist it
like a cinnamon bun,
then wind a ribbon
of palmetto between
each row. Next comes
the sweetgrass,
slender as thread.
You don't know how
strong it is till you
feed it through
the basket. You don't
know how strong
it is till you need it.

My grandmother taught me in the yard of her house on Route 17.
We sat in the shade of oak trees knitted together at the top like old
friends clasping hands. If I messed up, she'd rip it apart and make
me do it over till it was perfect—"up tuh de notch," we say in
Geechee. Some days you work till sunlean just to end up where you
started.

For contrast, use
bulrush grass, like
the basket that kept
baby Moses safe:
"When she could
hide him no longer,
she took for him
a basket made
of bulrushes
and daubed it with
bitumen and pitch.

She put the child
in it and placed it
among the reeds
by the river bank."

Cars would stop at our roadside stand, and we'd run inside yelling,
"Granny, you got a sale! You got a sale!" She'd come out of the
kitchen drying her hands on a dishtowel.

Baskets for bread, fruit,
vegetables, and eggs.
Baskets for shrimp
and crabs. Baskets for
laundry and sewing.
Baskets for packing
lunches. Baskets
for picking cotton.
Placemats, hot pads,
basinets, jewelry, hats,
offering pans for church.

Breathe it. Breathe it in. Sweetgrass smells like summer. Like
summer rain. Like summer rain in the Lowcountry.

Pinus acus.
Sabal etonia.
Muhlenberia filipes.
Juncos roemerianus.

My grandmother said the white man brought us here because he
didn't know how to grow rice. He needed our people to teach him.
He needed our people to make the baskets for the harvest. You put
the rice in the basket and jostle it good to loosen the chaff. It comes
off easy like skin. Like real thin skin.

Weavers work
the grass with
sharp tools:
filed-down nails,
spoons, or the rib
bone of a pig.

*The thing of it is, you might think you know what you're going
to make, but the basket has its own ideas. It talks to you. You just
have to listen.*

Call it a bone
even when it's
not made of bone.
Even when it's
forged from iron
or steel. Even
when it's plastic.
Call it a bone.

*I taught my daughter and my granddaughters, too. I say, "Take
your time—you want a well-made basket, not a hurry basket."*

I am here with my own daughter.
She wasn't supposed to be with me
this week. She was supposed to be
on a class trip to a foreign city.
But as she waited to board her plane,
a man in that city drove his anger
into a crowded street, mowing down
children and families who were
licking ice cream cones as fireworks
splashed against the black sky.

*At recess, we'd practice on whatever grass we could find in the
schoolyard. It was the Old Gregory School in Mount Pleasant. We
had to bring our own wood to keep warm in the winter.*

I know how this sounds: poor, poor
white girl and her canceled trip
to Europe. It's true. Or true enough.
Except: my children are dark.
Dark enough to be asked—
on outings with their pale mother—
if they're adopted. Dark enough
to have a biracial woman
think they're biracial. Dark enough
to have a cop pull my son over
for no reason and scream
at him, neck bulging with rage,
until I rolled down the tinted back
window to ask, "What's the problem,
officer?" Flustered, he said,
"I don't have time for this"
and sped away. On the ride home,
I sat on my hands to stop them
from shaking.

They brought my great-great-great-great-great-great grandfather
from Angola to Sullivan's Island. Nothing but a sign there now.
Middle Passage.

I did not plan to write about
my daughter. I did not plan
to write about my son.

He was a boy. A strong boy but still just a boy, Granny told me.
She heard it from her mamma who heard it from her own mamma,
and so on.

Here is the grass.
Here is the basket.
Here is the stitching.
Here is the child.
Here is the river.

Here are the reeds,
rustling. Listen. Listen.

Notes

"Rana Plaza": A building housing five factories in Savar, Bangladesh collapsed on April 24, 2012, killing nearly one-third of the 3,600 textile workers.

The "HR Erasure" series poems are based on various employee handbooks and human resources manuals.

As subcontractors of Hill Country Farms, a branch of Henry's Turkey Service, the men depicted in the "The Boys from Atalissa" were subjected to squalid living quarters, brutal working conditions, and verbal and physical abuse until social service agencies intervened in 2009. The case led to the largest jury verdict in EEOC history. All of the information from the "Company Manual" sections is from the "Hill Country Farms Program Description," November 1, 1980. The manual was known within the company as "The Magic of Simplicity." Some of the details and information from the poem were gathered from articles published in *The New York Times* and *The Des Moines Register*.

The names in "Indigo" are from memorials to enslaved people at the Whitney Plantation in Wallace, Louisiana.

"Ike Turner's Obituary" is an erasure of an excerpt of the obituary for Ike Turner published in *The New York Times* on Dec. 13, 2007. The poem was written in response to the numerous obituaries for Tina Turner in 2023 that referenced her having been "discovered" by Ike Turner, her abusive ex-husband.

"What Did You Do Last Week" is based on an email Elon Musk sent to millions of federal workers in late February 2025 demanding that they submit a report on five things they did the previous week or face losing their jobs.

Acknowledgments

The following poems appeared originally in the following journals, sometimes with different titles or formatting:

"Rana Plaza" in *Women's Studies Quarterly*

"Imperial Valley" in *Southern Humanities Review*

"Midterm" in *North American Review*

"Schuhläufer" in *Glass* poetry journal

"Nothing to Trade" in *Rabbit* (Australia)

"HR Erasure: Policy on Clarity," "HR Erasure: Policy on Manager Responsibilities," and "HR Erasure: Policy on Drug and Alcohol Use" in *Scoundrel Time*

"Vultures" in *Poets Reading the News*

"Search & Rescue" in *Arkana*

"Shitshow" in *Action, Spectacle!*

"Transactions," "Elegy for the 30-Year Career," and "The Doorkeepers" in *The Summerset Review*

"My Neighbor the Egg Inspector" in *Pittsburgh Poetry Review*

"You Break It, You Bought It: A Villain-elle" in *One Art*

"What Did You Do Last Week?" in *The New Verse News*

"Nothing to Trade" was a longlist finalist for the National Poetry Society Prize, United Kingdom.

Special thanks to Tony Perez and Corrie Ferguson of the Emma Barrientos Mexican American Cultural Center in Austin, Texas, for their assistance with research for this manuscript.

Thank you to the Penn State Altoona Advisory Board for funding to conduct research.

Thank you to the Humanities Institute at Penn State University for funding to conduct research.

About the Author

Erin Murphy is the author or editor of more than a dozen previous books of poetry and prose, most recently *Fluent in Blue*. Her work has appeared in *Ecotone, Rattle, Women's Studies Quarterly, The Best of Brevity, Best Microfiction 2024,* and anthologies from Random House, Bloomsbury, Bedford/ St. Martin's. Her awards include a Dorothy Sargent Rosenberg Poetry Prize, two Foreword INDIES Book of the Year awards, and a Best of the Net award. She is professor of English at Penn State Altoona and poetry editor of *The Summerset Review*. Website: www.erin-murphy.com

www.ingramcontent.com/pod-product-compliance
Lightning Source LLC
Chambersburg PA
CBHW021123130626
46554CB00002B/837